POETRY
FOR THE *Soul*

Volume 1

POETRY FOR THE *Soul*

Volume 1

Prose from the Heart

Janice Stampley Means

iUniverse, Inc.
Bloomington

Poetry for the Soul: Volume 1
Prose from the Heart

iUniverse books may be ordered through booksellers or by contacting:

iUniverse
1663 Liberty Drive
Bloomington, IN 47403
www.iuniverse.com
1-800-Authors (1-800-288-4677)

ISBN: 978-1-4759-7148-4 (sc)
ISBN: 978-1-4759-7149-1 (ebk)

Printed in the United States of America

iUniverse rev. date: 01/09/2013

POETRY FOR THE SOUL
Prose from the heart

DEDICATION

TO MY LORD AND SAVOIR JESUS CHRIST
"I thank you for blessing me to be one of yours"

TO MY LOVING FAMILY
&
THE LATE HARDY AND DOROTHY STAMPLEY

CONTENTS

"THE HEALER"

I tell people at this point in my life
I don't worry about having surgery
or going under a knife
Because once I've prayed right then I understand
That my healer will touch the surgeons hands
So when the surgeon lays his hands on me
I'm assured he's been given everything he needs
And God promised he wouldn't leave
me so when I close my eyes
I know that my healer is by my side
But the reason I'm not scared to go under a knife
Is because my healer is the same one who gave me life
So when I undergo surgery I go to my healer and say
Touch the hands of the surgeon that
will perform my surgery today
Because we have to realize that the surgeon is just a man
But the healer is the one who holds
all power in his hands.

"AWESOME VOICE"

During my life I endured the kind of pain
That would've drove the average person in sane
But God allowed me to go through test after test
Because he knew it was my season to be blessed
I felt like Job when he was all alone
Because my children was defiant
and my husband was gone
But one night while I was sitting at home
I was taken by the spirit into another zone
And all of a sudden I heard a voice in my head
And I grabbed a pen and paper to
write down what he said

He said "I was a born conqueror in Christ
And that this would be the turning point in my life
And ever since that awesome day
That voice in my head has never went away
But now I know the reason for the
things that I went through
It was so I could have testimonies
for what I was about to do
That's why in this season everything that I write
Will be an inspiration to someone's life
So when people ask me "What inspired me to write?"
I tell them "It was that awesome voice
of God in the middle of the night"

"FORGIVE ME"

Please forgive me for what I'm about to do
But I've decided to stop waiting on you
I've been there for you as long as I can
And I hope that one day you'll understand
I gave you the best years of my life
And you still neglected to treat me right
I stuck by you through thick and thin
But now it's time for this cycle to end
You took it for granted I'll always be there
But now I've found someone who truly cares
Forgive me if I'm hurting you but I'm hurting too
Because I wasted so many precious years with you
But most of all forgive me for the pain
you're about to go through
When you realize I'm no longer there for you
You'll always hold a place in my heart
But this is where the cycle ends
and my new life can start

"GIVING UP"

We all make decisions whether they're wrong or right
But I made one that saved my life
But let me explain why I said it that way
So you'll understand better what I'm about to say
God blessed me to marry a very humble man
But at the same time the devil had other plans
My husband did everything I asked him to do
But he allowed the devil to use him too
His addiction had gotten worse every day
And for years all I did was cry and pray
Because whenever I thought about giving up
He would reach out to me and that only made it tough
But one day I heard my youngest son say
That he was tired of seeing me living this way
But I stayed and endured the abuse more and more
Until the day I saw myself bleeding on the floor
God allowed this hardship to make sure I knew
That if I didn't give up now I'd die from physical abuse

"GRIEVING"

When a loved one dies people tend to take it hard
And some go as far as blaming it on the Lord
But we all have a designated time
That we too must cross that line
So don't let someone's death make you bitter and cruel
Because there's a reason for everything that God do
And there's nothing that anyone can say or do
To change what God has planned for you
And I realize God makes no mistakes
I even got mad when he took my mother away
But he took my mother so I could see
That life isn't easy as I thought it would be
Because if she hadn't died my life wouldn't be the same
And I wouldn't have these testimonies
to glorify his name
So grieve if you may but not too long
Because only God knows the day and
time we all must come home

"SCANDALOUS"

When you've been there for a person
through thick and thin
It hurts to find out you have a scandalous friend
I remember my friend use to come to my house
When she thought no one was there but my spouse
When we was together she always acted the same
But when my spouse was around her
whole demeanor changed
And every time she came by she wore short clothes
So that some part of her body would always be exposed
I didn't want to believe it even though there were signs
Because I didn't think my friend would cross the line
So shortly afterwards I talked to my spouse
And he said she had winked at him one day at the house
And I asked him "Why didn't you tell me right then"
And he said "I felt awkward and
besides she's your friend"

At that very moment I decided to see
If she could do something so scandalous to me
So immediately after I set a trap
And doubled back to find her on my doormat
So women stop thinking it's always the men
Because sometimes you just have a scandalous friend

"BEAUTY"

If I was asked to characterize a tree
I wouldn't go by what I see
Because what looks good on the
outside can bare bad fruit
And the same thing applies to me and you
That's why I never judge a person from what I see
Because I believe beauty is what's underneath
If you visualize a moth it's ugly on the outside
But once it develops it's a beautiful butterfly
We can change our outer appearance
but we're still the same
Because in Gods eyes the only difference is our name
People always think that they don't look right
But when God created us he said "We
were beautiful in his sight"
We all have battle scars that change our outer view
But the real beauty shows when you bare good fruit

"A HUG"

When you're around a person that's mad every day
There may be a reason why they're acting that way
I recall one day I was sitting at work
Having pity for myself and feeling hurt
I called a co—worker to my station that day
Not knowing what I was about to say
When she came and saw no one around
I told her "I had called her down"
I said "No one wants to be my friend"
And she said "Maybe it's the kind of message you send"
But when she saw I was hurting she gave me a hug
And tears came to my eyes from her showing me love
And it dawned on me what was missing in my life
Because it only took a hug to make everything alright
And every day after that she gave me a hug
To keep me reminded that I was loved
And now my life's changed in so many ways
And it's all because of a hug I received that day

"BROKEN"

It takes time to heal when someone's done you wrong
Because your heart's been broken and you're all alone
And even though you had intentions to please
He still felt it was time to leave
He decided to leave while you was at work
Not even considering how much you would hurt
He had you at the point where you didn't know what to do
And that was the worst kind of mental abuse
He humiliated you and tore you down inside
And even tried to strip you of your pride
He proved he didn't care about you and the kids
When he was able to walk away like he did
But now he's sorry and wants to come back
But God has other plans than that
Because you still haven't healed to this day
From the pain he caused when he walked away
And even though he left you hurt and confused
God still made a way out of no way for you

He lifted the broken spirit that was left behind
And healed your broken heart and gave you peace of mind
He's opened doors to supply all your needs
And all he wants is you to have faith and believe
So just stay strong throughout it all
Because God will be your strength after the fall

"BETRAYAL"

I felt the need to let you know
How your betrayal has hurt me so
I know our love has faded away
But there's some things the heart won't let the mind erase
You started sneaking around and trying to hide
And when I asked "Was you cheating?"
you chose to tell me lies
And even though I knew what you had planned
I respected my vows and didn't turn to another man
We made a promise that if we should ever part
That neither of us would break the other's heart
But because of your betrayal our
marriage was torn apart
And you didn't even care that it was breaking my heart
And on top of humiliating me and
deliberately telling me lies

When I found out who she was I could have litterly died
For how you hurt my heart there was no excuse
Because the pain I felt was the worst kind of abuse
I hope you never experience the humiliation and hurt
Of having a broken heart while you're at work
You left me with a pain that was so severe
That if it wasn't for my children I
wouldn't of had the will to live
You could never understand what it took each day
For me to go to work and put a smile on my face
But the day I decided to walk out that door
Was the turning point because I couldn't take no more
But I felt you could've done things in a different way
Because I didn't deserve to be humiliated and betrayed

"A UNION"

We honor the Holy Spirit, the Father and the Son
Today you come as two but you'll leave as one
God has filled this house and blessed this room
With a handsome and beautiful bride and groom
A marriage is a union full of happiness & joy
So when you say "I do" let it be for love
So starting right now and until the end
Your partner will now become your best friend
And today your lives will forever change
Because you will be carrying his last name
And now that you've grown together in Christ
You're about to be united as man and wife
And from this day forward you should honor in your heart
The vow God made "Till death do us part"

And if you honor the vows that you make here today
God will bless this union in a mighty way
You've come a long way since you first met
And your love has endured many tests
The person before you will be your partner for life
So submit to your husband and you to your wife
And as you stand here today exchanging
vows from the heart
Let what God put together no man take a part
And the strength of the Lord will be your help
As long as God is ordering your steps

"THE REASON"

Every poem I've written glorifies
God in a miraculous way
But none compares to the miracle
that stands before you today
Just me standing here with cuts on my throat and face
Is reason enough for me to give God the praise
If it wasn't for God shedding his mercy and grace
I wouldn't have this joy that I feel today
Because when I was bound and not living right
My testimonies is what made me change my life
Because I could've been lying six feet under the ground
But God had a reason for keeping me around
That's why I'm always ready and willing to serve
Because God didn't give me what I deserved
But the reason I'm writing these poems about myself
Is so hopefully my trials can help someone else

"STANDING ON FAITH"

No matter what you're going through
There's someone having it worse than you
I remember one day I was talking to a friend
Telling him about the situation I was in
And as I was giving him some Godly advice
He started telling me what was happening in his life
And I realized that he was hurting inside
Because the pain and desperation showed in his eyes
He told me his bills were already late
And he was trusting in God and standing on faith
Then he said "He'd rather have the problems I do
Instead of all the problems he's going through"
By listening to him I thought to myself
I had forgotten from whom I get my help
So when I'm going through I just stand still and wait
And keep trusting in God and standing on faith

"FAMILY"

Families should have a close relation
Regardless of their situation
They should stick together through thick and thin
And support one another till the very end
And they should never have to bargain or plea
Just to get help in their time of need
Because by showing them they're not alone
Shows the unity in the home
There will be families that's humble and polite
While others have strife and do nothing but fight
And you shouldn't get jealous from what they may get
Because by trying to compete you'll only end up in debt
But if families stick together whether right or wrong
It could make their family tree grow strong
Because a family that prays together stays together too
So you pray for me and I'll pray for you

"PARENTS"

This day and time things are so confused
The children are telling their parents what to do
Each parent is responsible for their own child
But instead our children are running wild
And how can we tell them sleeping around is wrong
When they're watching their parents
bring someone home
But parents can't tell their children what to do
Because they're still trying to be young too
And the devil is crafty in all that he do
That's why he made adult clubs and kiddy clubs too
But the parents need to start back acting their age
And teaching their children how to behave
Because parents will lose all control in the end
If they don't stop trying to be their child's friend

"TWICE"

When I was in Mississippi I was cut in a fight
But I never imagined the same thing could happen twice
But after I got well I moved to another town
And found it was harder with no
family or friends around
And after running out of money for rent & food
I had to figure out what I was going to do
But then one day a guy was standing in my yard
And he told me "He noticed I've been having it hard"
He said "If I was willing I could make
some money on the side"
And because I was desperate I decided to try
It worked out fine for a little while
But I didn't feel right hustling around my child

It didn't feel good because I knew it wasn't right
To be selling a substance that was
destroying someone's life
But to make a long story short I
was robbed and cut again
But now I know the message that
God was trying to send
Things happen for a reason in everyone's life
But I never imagined I'd get my throat cut twice
But my scars are a testimony from where I came
And the fact I'm still living only glorifies Gods name

"BROKEN HEART"

I never knew how a broken heart felt
Until I had the chance to experience it for myself
But I didn't know my boyfriends' feelings had changed
Until I saw him with a girl after a football game
We had an argument the night before
And he said "It's probably best if we
don't see each other anymore"
But I brushed it off because I knew he was mad
And besides I was the only girlfriend he'd ever had
But when I saw them it hurt me so bad inside
That I ran to the parking lot and started to cry
I should've confronted him but I went home instead
And turned on some music and laid across my bed
It felt like my heart was being pulled through my skin
And that's something I never want to feel again
And now that I know how a broken heart feels
I can understand why it takes so long to heal

"CASUAL SEX"

When God created Adam & Eve he also created sex
But it wasn't meant to be used unless it was blessed
But the devil used Gods creation
in a totally different way
Because he had to find a way to get people to disobey
That's why he made sex the most pleasurable sin of all
Because he knew it was a sure way
to get Gods people to fall
But since most people have had sex
at some point in their life
The devil is pleased because he's
keeping them from living right
And casual sex is fun especially when you're young
But it gets more serious the older you become
And having casual sex is normally what you'll do
To get back at someone for cheating on you
But there's too many diseases going around
From people having casual sex all over town
Because when they use their bodies they just don't know
They're giving the devil power over their soul
So don't use your body because that's where God dwells
And allow casual sex to send you to hell

"DIVORCE"

A divorce can be a devastating thing to go through
Especially if it's not what both spouses want to do
Divorce is probably a person's worst fear
After being together for many years
Because during a divorce you'll get angry inside
When you realize all this time you've been living a lie
And even though your marriage has fallen apart
You try to be careful about hurting their heart
But whenever you're talking to them on the phone
They try to make you feel like you're doing them wrong
But there's no more to say and they need to understand
Divorce is the only option and they're
not getting another chance
But the reason that people take divorce so hard
Is because a vow has been broken
that was honored by God

"HOMEGOING"

This is not a funeral it's Gods revelation
So rejoice because this is a celebration
The time has come for her to lay down and rest
But please don't cry because she's passed life's test
She accomplished everything that God required her to do
And she lived a righteous life just like he wanted her too
She had love in her heart for everyone
And she raised her children now her work here is done
All her loved ones should wipe their weeping eyes
We should be rejoicing there's no need to cry
God has stopped her pain and suffering and set her free
Now she's in a place of eternal peace
She's been taken out of this world of sin
But this is the beginning it is not the end

I know everyone is sad that she's gone
But she's with Jesus and she'll never be alone
She'll be walking around with a smile on her face
Praising God every step of the way
She'll be missed but she'll never be far
As long as we carry her in our hearts
We won't say goodbye because the day will come
When she'll rejoice and receive us with open arms
So don't remember her as she lay here today
She would want us to remember her in a happy way
God has freed her soul and taken her home
And Paradise Island is where she'll roam
She'll be looking at the sea and sitting in the sand
Waiting to be united with her loved ones again

"SICKNESS"

When I was young I can recall one day
Looking at my sister in a frightful way
Because as we were playing by the bed
I began to see a swelling on her head
I started screaming because I didn't know what to do
And I ran and got my mother so she could see it too
My mother asked my sister "What was wrong?"
And immediately dialed 911 on the phone
I didn't know bad things happened to someone little
But when I saw her again she was in the hospital
My mother and the doctor was talking one day
And she started crying and began to pray
She asked God "If it's in his will
Would he please let her baby live?"
And throughout her sickness my
mother reached out to God
And stepped out on faith even though it was hard
She proved she didn't depend on the doctors anymore
When she went to the healer and laid on the floor
And because of her prayers my sister still lives
And every day we thank God for keeping her in his will

"LONELINESS"

Loneliness is an emotion you feel when you're alone
And I'm experiencing loneliness right now at home
Because if no communication or
affection is being shown
You're living in a house because love is in a home
My spouse was locked up and I was left alone
And if I was to leave him he'll think I did him wrong
They say "You find a good thing when
you find yourself a wife"
But shouldn't the wife also have a good thing for life?
God said he'll never leave me and I know this to be true
But my spouse is my other half
shouldn't he be with me too?
I know I'm not alone because I'll always have you
But my flesh is getting weak and it desires attention too
And what if my spouse keeps going to jail
Do I suppose to be lonely and do the time as well?
No one wants to go through life being lonely all the time
Because just sitting at home can
make you lose your mind
Lord move this lonely feeling that I have inside of me
And let the Holy Spirit give me the comfort that I need

"BOUND"

When you have loved ones that's
allowed themselves to be bound
You hope nothing has happened when
you don't see them around
You want to talk to them but don't know where to begin
Because they've gotten caught up in a world of sin
Their friends and family no longer come around
And their hanging with people that's
gonna keep them bound
Even when God sends a shepherd their way
The first thing they'll do is run away
That's because the devil's controlling their minds
And he's tricked them and told them to run and hide
But everyone's been bound in one way or another
So we should keep praying for our sisters and brothers
Because when a person's bound I
found one thing to be true
If someone gives up on them they'll
discourage others too
People always say they've done the best they can
But Jesus got beat to his death and
never gave up on man

"SAVED"

When you stand before God and proclaim to be saved
You must be ready to change your ways
Because once you proclaim that you're living for the Lord
Everything in your life will start getting hard
And when you went down in Jesus name
You proved you were serious about making a change

And the enemy has traveled very far
To see if you're who you say you are
And if he can get you to curse Gods name
He'll prove to God that you haven't changed
So expect the worst when you get saved
Because the enemy will attack you every day
And the attacks will get harder every time
But you'll reap your reward on down the line
So by living your life in a Godly way
Proved you was ready when you proclaimed to be saved

"A GOOD MAN"

The women of today don't understand
What it takes to find a good man
We can pray for a good man all our life
And soon as we get one; we won't treat him right
And because we're worried about what people will say
We want them to look and be built a certain way
And since the enemy knows what you want too
He'll end up sending a decoy to you
And he'll send you place's like the clubs
Knowing that clubs only have thugs
And one sign I've seen of an ungodly man
Is when they're walking around in sagging pants
But you'll know when a good man comes your way
Because you'll get confirmation from what he do and say
And a good man will keep a smile on your face
And he'll call and compliment you every day
So focus on their heart and see if it's true
Because a good man could be right in front of you

"ABUSED"

There's so many women that's been abused
And now they've become scared and confused
But let me share something about myself
Because after being abused I had nothing left
Throughout my life I've been abused in ways
That some women would be shame to say
And even though I hated living this way
I allowed him to dictate what I did and say
And because I was scared of what he might do
I allowed him to abuse my children too
Because when I didn't stand up for myself
He knew I couldn't stand up for anyone else
And I always cried when I had to submit
Because after being abused sex will make you sick
And he didn't even act like he was aware
That the love we once had was no longer there
And every day I just wondered when
This nightmare would come to an end

"SECRETS"

Everyone has a secret they've held inside
But there are some secrets we shouldn't try to hide
And some people have secrets
they've kept to themselves
Because they've been abused and told not to tell
But most kept secrets can tear your life apart
Because they are secrets that's crucial to your heart
But what happens in the dark will come to the light
So if they say it's a secret you'll
know something's not right
But there's no secret that people can hold
Because the one that sees all sits high and looks low
And if you tell God a secret that's as far as it goes
But if you tell anyone else expect
the whole world to know
So when you confess your secrets even
though God already knows
You're giving it to the maker and
being healed by letting it go

"OVERCOMER"

I'm here today as an overcomer myself
Because I know how it feels to reach out for help
If I hadn't tried to find a way to leave
There was a possibility he would've killed me
So one day I decided to leave my spouse
But only for him to drag me back to the house
Because of his addiction he wouldn't let me go
And I was too embarrassed to let my family know
He would come through the windows late at night
Now imagine being awakened by that kind of fright
And none of your men may have ever went as far
As kicking and beating you and dragging you with a car
And after putting me through all this hell
His only punishment was going to jail
But even though he abused me and did me wrong
It still was hard for me to leave him alone
But I cleared my head and started going to church
And stay prayed up and watched God work
And now I've overcome the heartaches and pain
And if you give it to Jesus you can do the same

"MOTHER KNOWS"

When I was a teenager my mother use to say
To cherish my body and don't give it away
Because a man will tell you whatever it takes
To get you to make that one mistake
And he'll make you think you're doing him wrong
By making him have to wait so long
But there's no excuse if he gets under your clothes
Because he can't go any further than you allow him to go
Because once he gets you to cross that line
He'll think he can come back anytime
And after he's worn your body down
He'll spread your name all over town
So hold on to the jewels that you posses
And always remember that mother knows best

"FIRST LOVE"

It's hard to forget the first love of your life
Because everything in your world feels so right
When they came around your heart would beat fast
Because they were your first, middle and last
And your emotions were never the same
Because you'd get excited just by hearing their name
And they promised never to break your heart
So you didn't let anyone keep you apart
You told them secrets that no one else knew
Because you thought your love was true
And the feelings you had in your heart was so strong
That in your mind they could do no wrong
But down the line you started to see
The relationship you cherished wasn't meant to be
But there's never a time that I can think of
That I didn't think about my first love

"HELL"

The bible tells us in the book of revelation
That hell is the pit that holds all generations
People mostly talk about heaven and the seals
But the fiery pits of hell is also real
If the devil can get you to hold sin within
Hell is the place where you will end
Some people say "You don't go to hell
just because you're not in church
But regardless if you don't go to church;
"What about your faith and works?"
God said "Faith without works is dead"
So either you're going to heaven or hell instead
Because when people do wrong on a worldly realm

They know there's such thing as a jail
But when they do wrong on a spiritual realm
Then why don't they believe there's a hell?
I've always wondered why people say
When someone dies they're going to a better place
Everyone don't make it to heaven
that's something we all know
So if they don't go to heaven then "Where do they go?"
I know this may be deep and hard to understand
But just like God created heaven
hell was part of his plan
A thousand years has passed and Satan is out to devour
And all the unbelievers will burn in a lake of fire

"SIN"

When you've done something you know is a sin
Then what makes you keep doing it over again?
We all knew since the beginning of time
The devil made it seem like sinning was fine
And by the devil being crafty in all that he do
If he can get you to sin; he'll make a mockery out of you
Because the bible said "When this world begin
The devil was kicked out of heaven because of sin"
That's why sins designed to be something we like
Because the more we sin; the further
we're taken from Christ
So if you receive a gift from one of your friends
Don't consider it a blessing if it's obtained through sin
Because God will give you things to fulfill your needs
But if it's obtained through sin the
devils behind the scene
And because this battle will be long and hard
We have to be careful about sinning against God
And if we love the Lord we'll restrain from sin
And that'll keep the devil from winning in the end

"RACISM"

Ever since I was a little girl
Racism has been in this world
But I promised myself that I would never be
The type of parent to force racism on my seed
It shocked me when my son came to me one day
And asked "Would it be alright to date
a person of another race?"
I told him "Yes, if that's what he wants to do
Because their race doesn't matter
as long as they love you"
Because one thing I know is love will conquer all
And if people stop looking at color racism will fall
And by me not showing racism my
two sons are doing the same
And if all parents practice this; it could
be the beginning of a racial change

"EVERYTHING"

After all I've been through during my life
I finally met a man that treated me right
We was introduced at a cookout one day
And he smiled at me in a flirty way
I wasn't dating at the time
Because I had more important things on my mind
It flattered me when he called that day
And he also impressed with what he had to say
He asked "Could we go somewhere and talk"
And I told him "I would give it some thought"
We agreed on a movie later that day
And he treated me like a lady every step of the way
And ever since we went on that date
We both realized it must've been fate
His every touch felt like a dream come true
And it shocked me to hear him say "I love you"
I realized our meeting was in God's plan
Because he's everything I ever wanted in a man
And I know that when the time is right
I'll be more than honored to become his wife

"HOMOSEXUALITY"

Men and women today are trying their best
To get us to condone being with the same sex
Because when you look around all you can see
Is women walking around with their pants to their knees
And there's something in the lives
of men's that's missing
When you see them walking around
plucking and twisting
And even though it's been going on since biblical times
The bible never condoned that this behavior was fine
Because in the bible it specifically reads
"That God created Adam and Eve"
Because he knew only a man and woman could comply
When he said "Be fruitful and multiply"
But we can't talk about them or treat them cruel
Because that's not what God wants us to do
Because they could've been hurt or even abused
Or maybe they're just sexually confused
That's why we should minister and try not to judge
Because homosexuality can be overcome by love

"ENOUGH"

During my marriage I endured so much pain
Until sometimes I felt like I was going insane
But when we first met I never saw a sign
That he was capable of hurting me down the line
But all I wanted during that time
Was to be happy and have a peace of mind
But instead my life became unhappy and confused
And by staying in the marriage I was also abused
He stopped coming home for days at a time
And when he did; he acted like everything was fine
It felt like a nightmare and I wanted to die
But God picked me up and said
"Wipe your weeping eyes"
"The time has come when enough is enough
And it's time to make a decision even
though it may be tough"
So I started seeking God every day and night
Until I started seeing a change happen in my life
And now I'm getting stronger every day
Because when God said "Enough" my
whole situation went away

"DISTANT"

Our daily lives keep us on the run
And it hinders us from seeing our loved ones
It took someone to die for us to see
That we're not as close as we should be
By the time we come together most
of our children are grown
And can't recognize one another
from being apart so long
But you can always tell when everyone is in town
Because throughout the house
you'll hear a joyous sound
And while the adults are catching
up on what they've done
The children get together and plan them some fun
And you'll start reminiscing about your past
It may have been bad but it still makes you laugh
But now the trip is coming to an end
And a feeling of sadness has started kicking in
Even though you're not ready it's time that you go

That's when everyone gets together
and plan to stay close
But it's hard to hold back tears and try to be strong
When you don't know when you'll see
them again once they're gone
But there's one thing God has allowed me to see
And that's the love we have in our family tree

"I WISH"

A Dedication to my mother

I miss you mama and I wish you could see
How I've grown into the woman you wanted me to be
And even though you're in a better place
I still wish that God hadn't taken you away
And I wish you was here so you could see
How I applied to my life what you installed in me
Sometimes I see visions of you in my dreams
And I know in my heart you're watching over me
I never realized what I was putting you through
Until now, because I'm going
through the same things too

You always told me to do the best I can
So I would never have to depend on a man
But now that God's supplying all my needs
I won't need a man to take care of me
Whenever I think of you I begin to shed tears
Because I didn't appreciate you while you was here
But I've learned to cherish each moment as I go
Because once it's gone you can't rekindle it anymore
But most of all you taught me no matter what I gain
To never forget my family and from where I came

"NEXT GENERATION"

The children of today have started a new phase
They're trying to do things their own way
They've stop listening to what their parents say
They don't even respect that they're of old age
And they think we don't know what they need
But every day we're planting a seed
We want to bless them for things that they do
But we say "come at one" and they'll come at two
We tell them things that can help in their life
But before the conversation ends
we're wrong and they're right
And the devil is using them when they come to church
To interfere with Gods work
Regardless of their age they think they're grown
They even sit in church texting on their phones
We need to get our children back
serious about Gods word
So they'll be able to minister what they've heard
But the devils entering their minds anyway he can
Preferably through rap, cars, sex and dance
Because if he can stop the parent—child relation
He will control the next generation

"MISERY"

From six years ago today
God has brought me a mighty long way
I blamed God for what happened the day
He came and took my mother away
My heart had begun to feel numb and cold
It felt like ice was around my soul
I had so much anger built up in me
Till it felt like black was all I could see
I didn't care about no one whether white or black
It felt like the devil was on my back
But by the grace of God I went to church one night
Because I was ready to start living right
It's amazing after a period of time
How a person's trials can change their mind
Because I had to be cut up, beat down and abused
Before I made the decision to let myself be used
But first I had to start living right
So he could use my testimonies to change someone's life
And when everyone saw how I had changed
It made them praise and glorify Gods name
Because they all thought it was miraculous to see
The transformation of a sinner like me

"FRIENDS"

People are quick to say that someone's their friend
But shouldn't a friend be loyal to the end
A friend is there for you from the start
Because their sincerity comes from the heart
And a real friend don't want to see you stressed
And they'll celebrate with you when you're blessed
And you can tell them your deepest secrets
And won't hear it again for any reason
And when you need them they'll always come around
Because a real friend will never let you down
They'll tell you things they think you should know
Because they want to see your relationships grow
So unless they'll stand by your side to the end
You shouldn't consider them as your friend

"MOLESTED"

Every day people around the world
Are hearing about molested little boys and girls
That's because the parents of the children should take
The initiative to make sure they're in a safe place
Because adults can lead children in the wrong way
By coaxing them on what to do and say
Because in a child's mind they suppose to do
Whatever an adult ask them too
But children listen to what I say
No one is allowed to touch your private place
No matter if it's your parents, family or friends
If touched the wrong way there's a
message your body will send

Because there are some people that's sick in the mind
And get enjoyment from making children cry
And if they say it's a secret about
what you're going to do
That's the first sign that they're going to hurt you
So if someone tries to touch you in your private place
Make sure you go and tell someone right away
But if you've been molested you
haven't done anything wrong
But by talking about what happened
can help you to move on

HATERS

When the time comes you will know
Who the haters are that don't want to see you grow
You can tell when a hater come around
Because their purpose is to bring your spirit down
But God can place gifts in whoever he choose
So don't worry when your haters start talking about you
The reason I can stand in front of my haters and be bold
Is because God is my strength and he's in control
When God anoints a person with a certain task
Your haters will try to detour your path
People can laugh and talk to you every day
But as soon as you're blessed you'll
see the hate on their face
But I use my spirit of discernment so I can see
Who my haters are and whose celebrating for me
Because when God say he's for us
that's all we need to know
But we still need our haters because they help us grow
In order to know your haters just
tell them how you're blessed
And their facial expression and
attitude will tell you the rest

"SISTERLY LOVE"

Sisters are people who relate from the heart
They grow up feeling each other's pain from the start
Sisters can laugh and sisters can cry
But eventually one day
They'll have to say good bye
And even though they're far apart
They'll always hold memories deep in their hearts
They grew up living in the same home
And even though they had each
other they were still alone
Sisters share secrets that a brother wouldn't dare
That's why a sisterly love is oh so rare
Sister, sister our love is so deep
Now we can let our daughters make the cycle complete

A PERSONALIZED CARD
"TO SOMEONE SPECIAL"

Forgive Me

It's time we made amends because life is too short
So I'm asking you to forgive me for breaking your heart
These words I'm saying is probably hard to believe
Because I let you down in your time of need
I turned my back when you needed a friend
Not realizing it could cause our relationship to end
I know this card can't make the pain go away
But I'm asking you to forgive me for pushing you away

FINAL ATTEMPT

Over time I've noticed that life's unfair
Because it took the memories that we once shared
I can't believe I gave you my heart
Just for you to give it back after tearing it apart
I asked God to show me a sign from above
So I can know how to regain our love
And I've seen everything I needed to see
And I've come to the conclusion you no longer want me
And now that you're having a change of mind
It's putting our marriage on the line
I've done everything I could possibly do
To be a good wife like you wanted me too
You're breaking my heart more and more each day
And it's making it hard to keep a smile on my face
And whenever we're sitting around the house

I notice that we no longer talk
It's time this nightmare come to an end
Because we're in a marriage we're not just friends
And there's nothing else that I can say
But we can't continue living this way
But don't get me wrong I'm not blaming it all on you
Because I played a major role in it too
We made a vow till "Death do us part"
And I'm trying to find out what's in your heart
And now there's a decision that needs to be made
Like is our marriage over or can it be saved?
And I'm leaving this decision totally up to you
Because this is my final attempt to
see what you want to do

"A GOOD DAY"

My friend and I was arguing one day
And my co-worker had a worried look on his face
After telling him my problem I
asked "What should I do?"
And he said "The enemy will use the closest one to you"
And I said "He's not the closest and the devil is wrong
Because the closest one to me sits on the throne
And I won't allow my day to be bad for any reason
Because I'm too close to my blessing in this season"
And by me standing still he realized he was wrong
And later that morning he sent a text to my phone
He said "Even though this morning
I didn't have much to say
I still love you and have a good day"

"MY VISION"

When I was a little girl
My vision was to make a difference in this world
And now that I'm grown I can finally see
That all things are possible to those who believe
Every day I expect someone to come my way
Either to talk or just ask me to pray
They'll come to me because they can see
The anointing God has placed on me
And even though I have a small beam of light
The God in me shines high because
I'm trying to live right
So when God send someone to talk to me
He'll give me a word that can help set them free
And at the end of my vision when my work is done
I vision God saying "Well done daughter well done"

"A BORN CONQUEROR"

We are all conquers in Christ
Everything won't always be nice
We just have to take a stand
And focus on God and what's at hand
God made women to be strong and free
Men aren't the only ones called to the seat
We all have talents that's bigger than us
So we have to stand firm, be faithful and just trust
Some people feel like it's hard to pray
But take it from me "Prayer is the only way"
We all have problems that we hold inside
But don't you know "Your testimony
is what keeps you alive?"
And instead of waiting on the man on the throne
We find men who abuse us because
we don't want to be alone

We privately do things that's out of the will of God
And think it's alright because we
haven't got caught so far
But in the midst of your storm when
you've lost all your might
That's when God shows up like a mighty beam of light
He'll touch your inner spirit, your soul and your heart
And at that very moment the healing will start
So don't give up in the midst of your fight
Because you're a born conqueror who's living for Christ

"SCARS"

Down in Mississippi when I was a young girl
Something happened that changed my world
Me and a friend went to a club one night
And she got drunk and got in a fight
And because I was young and knew nothing about life
I decided to help her so I jumped into the fight
But something happened to my amaze
She left with no marks but I was cut in the face
While waiting on the ambulance I said "let me see"
And when I looked in the mirror I
couldn't believe that was me
For a minute my vision darkened
and I saw a tiny beam of light
That was a sign that God was with me that night
I had a cut in my head and a hole in my face
And a cut beside my windpipe and several other places
My friends came to see me when I got home

But I was too embarrassed and just wanted to be alone
I had to sleep sitting up because I couldn't lay in a bed
I had 96 stitches and plates between
my neck and my head
And even though I was young I made a decision that day
Not to have surgery even though the state would pay
While I was healing I asked God
"Why did he let me live?"
But because I didn't know him I
assumed it was part of his will
By the time I got well I had lost all self esteem
But one day I met this lady and she looked at me
She said "You're as blessed as you can be
Every time you look in a mirror you
should fall on your knees"
I believe these scars was kept on me
So God could use my body as a testimony

"QUESTIONS"

God gave us the bible as a guide to live
But how do we know we're lining up with his will
Forgive me Lord for questioning your word
But I need some clarity on what I've heard
And only you have the answers to what I need to know
Like should I stay in my marriage
or is it time to let it go?
I've waited patiently for so long
And now I'm ready to make a decision;
but I'm scared it may be wrong
Because the bible says "Till death do us part"
But what if he's abused me and I have a change of heart?
And it also says "Submit only to your spouse"
But what if your spouse chose to go outside the house?
And if he's constantly leaving me by myself
Is it wrong to desire companionship from someone else?
My flesh is getting weak because I'm all alone

But I'm still holding on because my spirit is strong
Even though I need these answers right away
I still want them answered in a Godly way
But there's one question that's been heavy on my heart
Is it in your will for us to be apart?
Because I don't want to make a decision from what I feel
And go against what you have for me in your will
But you've already given me my answer from heaven
When you confirmed my release in
1st Corinthians chapter 7

"FORGOTTEN"

During my marriage there came a time one day
That my husband and I had problems
and went our separate ways
But something happened that I couldn't believe
He started living with a woman and
had forgotten about me
During 14 yrs. of marriage he never
called me by my name
He always called me "Baby" and that has never changed
The day we got married he promised me his heart
So how could he forget the vow "Till death do us part?"
And even though he had an addiction
I still treated him the same
Because he was still the man that gave me his last name
No matter what we went through
I stuck by him all the way
So how could he forget his wife and
the children he helped raise?
When I heard that he was seeing
someone it hurt so bad inside

Because he always said "He loved me"
but now I see those were just lies
He had forgotten I was suppose to
be the only woman in his life
But instead he abused who God gave him as a wife
People from our church prayed for us every day
They prayed for his deliverance and
that God would make a way
But when he ignored our vows and
eventually broke my heart
He didn't realize that he was tearing our marriage apart
When days turned to months and
things started getting hard
I got stronger every day by depending on the Lord
Now our marriage is ending because
I was betrayed so long
And because he had forgotten about
the wife he left at home

"PRIVATE PROPERTY"

I made the decision to live my life right
Because I'm the property of Jesus Christ
I want go back to none of my old ways
No matter if the devil sends a test every day
And now when things go wrong in my life
I totally depend on Jesus to make it right
And before any formed weapon can get me down
Jesus will stop it and turn it around
Because Jesus said that "I'm too blessed
To be walking around depressed or stressed"
And the devil can't take my joy or love
Because I received that from my Savoir above
And because I use the bible as a guide to live right
Jesus has placed favor over my life
And even though this walk may be long and hard
Backsliding is an option I'll always avoid
One of the commandments says "Thou shall not lie"
So for God I live and for God I'll die!
And once you make the decision to live your life right
You'll also become the property of
our Savoir Jesus Christ

"JEALOUS"

People tend to make their own life hard
Because they've forgotten they have a jealous God
When they meet someone and fall in love
They'll put them before the man above
But once God sees what you're up too
He'll take that person away from you
And even when you're married it's for better or worse
And he won't even let you put your spouse first
And he can make you a millionaire today
And if you cherish money he'll take it away
Because the 1st commandment specifically reads
"You'll worship no other God before me"
And because God's jealous we have to follow his plan
By putting him before any material things or man

"MY TESTIMONY"

If people only knew half my story
Then they would know why I give God the glory
I went through the majority of my life
Doing as I pleased and not living right
I had no love for people and always
found someone to blame
And because I didn't know Jesus
confusion was my middle name
So many people came into my life
Some treated me wrong and some treated me right
But when the devils beat you down all your life
It's hard to believe Gods already paid the price
And even though I wasn't living right
God still had his hands on my life

I did lots of things that could've left me dead
But God felt the need to save me instead
But then one day I was hurting inside
And cried out to Jesus with tears in my eyes
I said "I'm so tired of being bound"
And that's when he turned my life around
But I've come a long way from being bound
And now he said "I'm fit to wear my crown"
So when people wonder why I have such a high praise
It's because God has brought me a mighty long way

"CONFESSION"

Lord I stand before you ashamed as I can be
I'm dirty inside out from my head to my feet
My spirit is bitter and my heart is cold
And my mind is so messed up till I
don't know which way to go
I lost my identity and everything else
When I gave up on you started
worshipping someone else
I see my life remaining the same
Because I've made no effort in trying to change

And I only have myself to blame
For the shame I've brought upon my name
And even though I'm out of control
I know there's still hope because the
devil don't have my soul
You said in your word if we come to you and confess
That you would forgive us even
though we're a filthy mess
I'm ready to come out of this world of sin
I know I don't deserve it but this isn't how it should end
So I surrender it all as I lay on my face
And thank you for showing me mercy and grace

"TESTIMONY"

Everyone has a testimony that God require them to do
What he has for me may not be for you
A testimony is just a way to glorify Gods name
It was never intended to make you shame
But there's no testimony that he will give you
That you aren't able to carry through
Everyone's testimony won't be the same
So while you're going through just
keep praising his name
And some testimonies may be harder for you
But he's just equipping you for what he needs you to do
And then he'll give you a ministry to do
So he can get his glory out of you
And by telling your testimony of what God has done
You're fulfilling the will of his only son

"QUEEN"

Women today have to understand
It's time to stop being manipulated by man
Instead of treating us like a queen
They're taking away our self esteem
If women weren't scared of living alone
They'd realize they could make it on their own
But men will mistreat us and do us wrong
Until we realize we're independent and strong
Because we can know that something isn't right
But won't question the reason he's hanging out all night
And we don't realize we're only hurting ourselves
When we allow our men to be with someone else
Because instead of finding out where he's been
We settle with him saying "He was with his friends"
But they wouldn't get away with what they do
If we didn't allow them too
But women are queens despite what men may say
Besides we birthed forth the human race
And after experiencing Gods love and being redeemed
You'll never accept less than being treated like a queen

"FREE"

Everyone should want to be free
No one wants to be in captivity
I remember the day I changed my life
From a lifetime of sin to living for Christ
I received a word in church one night
That would help in the start of my new life
That night I fell down on my knees
And cried out to Jesus "I want to be free"
Right then I knew I'd been touched by Christ
Because something swirled around
me like a whirlwind of light
A pressure lifted like never before
It was a sign I wasn't bound anymore
My flesh started to shed and my eyes began to gleam
Jesus had touched me and I'd been redeemed
He said if I praise him with all my might
That he would place favor over my life
That night I slept lying in his arms
Knowing the world could do me no harm
I still think about it to this day

How all my worries had been taken away
My spirit feels like a feather in the wind
Because I'm no longer bound by sin
He gave me joy and took away the pain
Now I'm at peace because my Savoir reigns
And for the first time in my life I can see
That my Savoir has set me free

"MY BLESSED SEASON"

I've endured many heartaches and passed many test
And now it's my season to be blessed
There's a spiritual calling that's been placed on me
Because I'm a willing vessel that's been set free
I don't worry about how my bills will get paid
Because god's never failed to make a way
And I can sit at home and look around my house
And smile and thank God that everything is paid off
And even though it's a recession I don't have it hard
Because a recession don't affect the children of God
And as long as I stay faithful and remain standing bold
God said "There's no gift that he'll withhold"
So all my haters can keep talking about me
Because what God has for me it is for me
And I won't turn back for any reason
Because I realize I'm in my blessed season

"MOTHERLY LOVE"

The day you were born I held you close to my heart
And from that moment on we were never apart
I treated you with such tenderness and care
Letting you know I would always be there
I watched you grow from a baby to a man
But now I have to put you in God's hands
You'll grow up and do whatever it takes
Only then you'll understand from
the mistakes that you make
One day down the road throughout your life
You'll probably settle down and find yourself a wife
But as for me I have to follow Gods plan
And stop treating you like a baby and let you be a man

"THE HEAD"

In the book of Genesis we all have read
That God said "Man will be the head"
But the first mistake made as we can see
Was when man didn't take his place in the garden of Eve
By not taking charge in the garden that day
Showed that women can stand in a man's place
But even though a man is the head of his house
God will sometimes have to anoint his spouse
Because if the man's steps aren't ordered by God
His wife will be anointed to step up and take charge
So whether a man is anointed or a woman instead
When the enemy attacks he always go for the head
Because the head teaches the family to testify

And if he kills the head the body will die
And the devil will use any tactic to win
And he proved that in the beginning with sin
But when a man is ready to take his rightful place
His wife should step aside and take her place as his mate
Because no matter how long a man is out of
his place; he still wasn't meant to be led
And Gods word will never change from
saying "Man will always be the head"

"THE LOSS OF A MOTHER"

The day I lost my mother
It felt like my world shut down
My heart was full of emotions
And I didn't want anyone around
I never thought I would see the day
That part of my life would fade away
I felt like I had no reason to live
But God said "You still have your testimony to give"
My mother had installed in me all that she could
The will to live a good life "Like a good mother should"
I miss her more and more each day
But the memories we shared will never fade away
But time has passed and I have to follow Gods plan
To run this race as best as a good soldier can

"BLESSED AND FAVORED"

There are many reasons how I know I'm blessed
And the first one is I'm no longer stressed
I'm blessed to have a job that I like to do
And with favor from God I have 2 vehicles too
And I've learned that it is never hard
To take care of something I receive from God
That's why I stopped worrying a long time ago
About things in which I have no control
Because god will bless you with all your needs
As long as you're living obediently
God has blessed me with food to eat
And clothes on my back and shoes on my feet
I'd like to have money to buy things I need
But I'd rather for Jesus to have favor on me
And I've always been taught when I help someone
To not expect something in return
Because when you have favor from man and God
Expect your blessings to come from above
And by looking at my life you should see
Not only am I blessed but God has favor on me

"THE CHURCH"

So many people come to church
Some are bound and some are hurt
Everyone you encounter in your life
Won't always be living right
We all say we're doing what God require us to do
But we have to remember the devil have a job too
I have heard so many people say
That the Saints are the ones not living the right way
God require Saints to live a certain way
Because someone is watching us every day
And they can see that the Saints
aren't living like they should
Because the majority of the time they're up to no good
They see you come to church and praise and shout
And later that night they see you hanging out
That's why the church is always criticized
Because the Saints are living these double lives
The word says "God will come to the church first"
That's because he will reveal everyone's worth
God require Saints to let their life be their guide
To get the people in the streets to come inside

But it's hard for the church to get the people to believe
When they're seeing the Saints doing as they please
Church isn't the place for sister and brothers in Christ
To come to and have in their hearts so much strife
When they come to church instead
of listening to the word
They're talking about each other and what they've heard
But I have learned that we should pray
For the ones that talk about us anyway
The Saints need to stop treating each other this way
Because we're all trying to make it to the same place
If we suppose to love God in spirit and truth
We can't continue to live anyway that we choose
So you can go from day to day
Claiming you're living the right way
But in the end your work will tell
If you will make it to heaven or hell
And don't get upset because I wrote these rhymes
It's only what god required of me
because we're running out of time

"ADDICTIONS"

People with addictions are just like you and I
The only difference between us and them
is they don't do theirs on the sly
We all have to follow Gods will no matter what it takes
Because one thing about it God makes no mistakes
You may have a testimony that you don't understand
But there's nothing God will put you through;
that he can't bring you out again
Because this is a test they'll have to go through
So step aside and let God work
and watch what he will do
And even though it's something they have to go through
It's not just for them but it's a test for you too
God will allow the devil to send many tests your way
But he won't make you endure more than you can take
Because in their minds they want to do right
But when they're alone the spirits take flight
They're minds are weak and they're out of control
They don't know exactly which way to go
It's hard to see them in so much pain
But everything we do to help seems to fall in vain
And people will try to place the blame
like God isn't in control

But we are human just like them
and we can't save their soul
We can watch them day by day and
nothing will ever change
Until they seek God for themselves
things will remain the same
No one knows how it truly feels to love
someone with an addiction
You'll soon start forgetting yourself; and
see yourself praying for someone else
Because all we can do is pray
That their addiction will go away
But they aren't the ones that's hurting you so
It's the demonic spirits that won't let them go
It keeps them confused and all alone
To the point they don't know how to come home
There will be days they'll start playing games
Because they need to convince you
that they have changed
Then some nights you'll receive phone calls
Asking you to come get them like
they've done nothing at all

But the more you endure the heartaches
the more you'll start to know
That they're aiming for deliverance
but God is making you grow
Then the time will come when
they'll have nowhere to go
But you can't turn your back on them
because they are still a soul
They're only running a race that God has preordained
And even though you feel ashamed you
still need to stand for their name
So don't talk about them or treat them cruel
Because they're just a weak vessel
that the devil decided to use
Just thank God he didn't choose you,
Because then you would be acting just like them too
So don't look down on someone's afflictions
Because everyone of us has had
some sort of an addiction

"ABUSE"

Most people will experience abuse
at some point in their life
So allow me to educate you as an abused wife
When you first date everything will be cool
But later on he'll start telling you what to do
And down the line the jealousy will begin
And he'll start saying "He don't
trust you with your friends"
Then you'll start saying" You need a little space"
And it'll result in an argument and
he'll slap you in the face
And then he'll say "He's not letting you go"
But you'll insist because you can't take it anymore
And now you've gotten scared and begin to cry
Because he's saying "He'll hurt you before
he'll see you with another guy"
And now you're at the point where
don't know what to do
Because he's being apologetic for
putting his hands on you
But it can't be fixed because the damage is already done
And even though you didn't see it
the abuse had already begun

You want to believe that his love is true
But it was mental abuse when he told you what to do
And you hoped that one day he would change his ways
But he was physically abusive when
he slapped you in the face
So now you're doing things you think he would like
But the way he's treating you just isn't right
You want a way out because you're hurting inside
But you cover it up by telling everyone lies
And you're hoping your family don't have a clue
But they know exactly what he's doing to you
But the sad thing is there's nothing they can do
Because it has to be a decision that comes only from you
Every day someone is being abused
And I don't want what happened to me to happen to you
Because let me tell you in case you don't know
It will only get worse on down the road
So don't think that one day everything will be alright
Because it's not worth taking a chance with your life
Abuse starts mental but ends in a physical form
And one wrong decision can cause us to lose a loved one

"SINGLE PARENTS"

Most people are raising children on their own
Because the other parent has left them alone
It doesn't matter if they're a woman or a man
They should take responsibility for the children they had
It's hard for single parents to get
their children to understand
That they're only one person and
their doing the best they can
And when you're a single parent
that's doing the job of two
You sometimes have to make the
rules and enforce them too
We also have to teach our children
how to have self-respect
Because if they don't respect themselves;
they can't respect anyone else
Because when it comes to girls a mother already knows
That when they start seeing boys
they'll get out of control
And when it comes to boys a mother
could never understand

What it takes to teach him how to become a man
And when other children get something
yours will want it too
But your child only has one parent and theirs have two
And single parents get lonely and
have needs of their own
But their children will think they're wrong
if they brought someone home
And it's hard to find someone who
you can talk to and be real
Because anyone you meet has to
accept it's a package deal
But it's a job dedicating your life to a daughter and a son
That's why a man shouldn't get credit
for what a woman has done
So I salute to all the people that's
raising children on their own
Because there's a lot you have to
endure in a single parent home

"GROWTH"

There was a season during my life
When I worked with a woman that had strife in her life
But during that time I was always sad
And she gave me encouraging words
so I wouldn't feel so bad
Even when I needed rides home at night
She would come and get me even
though she would gripe
But down the line I began to see
That she was no longer talking to me
I didn't understand what had broken our ties
All I could figure is someone was telling her lies
Every time she saw me she would roll her eyes
And I would roll mine back because of my pride

We eventually started arguing and almost had a fight
And I realized it was time to seek God that night
I hadn't talked about her or made her mad
So I couldn't understand why she treated me so bad
My pastor said "That I should plant a seed
And ask God to give her whatever she need
And when I started praying I did exactly that
And that's all it took to break the devils back
But because of the issues we held in our heart
The devil tried everything to keep us apart
But over time we became back friends
And God proved to everyone the devil didn't win
I made it through that season and now I know
That God was using her as part of my growth

"TEMPTATION"

Everyone will experience temptation in their life
It's only a test to see if you're living right
No matter if you're a woman, man, boy or girl
Temptation lingers around the world
The bible says before this world begin
The devil even tempted God with sin
But temptation is only a test
It's not intended to see whose best
Whenever there's something that you like to do
You can always expect the devil to tempt you
The devil isn't out to play no games
If you flunk your test he'll shame your name

I was tempted as a child
Because the devil knew I was running wild
He tempted me at a club one night
And I ended up getting cut in a fight
But I wasn't shocked I almost died that night
Because God was even tested; to
see if he was living right
When the devil tempted God for 40 days and 40 nights
Proves that we will be tempted all our life
Times are hard and the devil is out to win
And since he couldn't get us in the beginning
he's trying to get us in the end

"DISRESPECTFUL CHILD"

I can remember back when I was a child
Out of all my siblings I was the only one running wild
I use to hide when my brother came around
Because instead of being at school I was all over town
I disrespected my grandmother
even though it wasn't right
By hanging out all hours of the night
No one could tell me where I could go
Because I was totally out of control
But while in the streets trying to be cool
My grandmother was signing me up for reform school
So I decided it was best that I slow down

Because I didn't want her sending me out of town
But even though I was in the streets running wild
I wasn't messing with boys to end up with a child
But later on I got cut in a fight
And now I realize why I almost died that night
Because a disrespectful child will
never live out their days
And I ended up learning that the hard way
And even though God could've taken my life
He gave me another chance to get my life right
And despite my past it was in Gods will
To give a disrespectful child another chance to live

"MINISTRY"

Some people think a ministry is what you do in church
But a ministry is all about doing God's work
God will give everyone a ministry to do
But the ministry for me may not be for you
There's lots of ministries that God can call you too
But you'll know the one that's meant for you
Your ministry is the calling that's
been placed on your life
But before you can do it you have to be living right
But I've always found one thing to be true
You can't run away when God is calling you
So whatever ministry God gives you to do
Do the best you can and he'll see you through
Because you would be surprised at what you can do
When God has placed an anointing on you
I just hope the ministry he's placed in me
Will help set another soul free

"THE WALK"

Lord I want to walk with you in spirit and truth
I want to keep my focus only on you
But as long as my body is covered with flesh
There will be times I won't pass my test
But every day I'm striving to do
The best I can to stay close to you
This walk isn't easy it's really hard
Because the things we desire; are the
very things we should avoid
Now I know why people don't come to Christ
It's because they think we're living a boring life
But Lord no matter what anyone says
I know that you will make a way
I'll trust you every day of my life
That's why I'm striving to live my life right
Lord I want to make it to heaven and see
The holes in your hands and the nails in your feet
During this walk I've endured many trials
But none compares to you giving your only child

"UNITED"

I've had a hard life and you have too
And now I've been blessed to cross paths with you
Every time I prayed I asked God to send
Someone in my life that could be my best friend
I knew you was special right from the start
Because you tore down the walls surrounding my heart
And as time went on I fell in love with you
And it helped to know you loved me too
And when you asked will I marry
you and become your wife
That was the happiest day of my life
And our desire to be intimate even though it wasn't right
Only made us more impatient to become man and wife
And even though we endured some heartaches and pain
Neither of our feelings ever changed
And down the line when times get hard
We'll both have to put our trust in the Lord
And because of the love we share in our hearts
We vowed that no one would keep us apart
And now the ceremony is about to begin
And I'm waiting to be united with my best friend

"CONFUSION"

Confusion plays a part in everyone's life
Whether it's from bitterness, jealousy or strife
It seems like most people in this day and time
Keep confusion on their minds
Because you can just be sitting at home
And confusion can get started on the phone
Confusion starts from something you've heard
And 9 times out of 10 they haven't said a word
And jealousy is also how confusion begins
And the majority of the time it starts with your friends
Sometimes you may wonder why
everyone's focused on you
But some people are bound and
have nothing better to do
When people see you're happy they'll
send confusion your way
Just for the purpose to mess up your day
And the devil will also send confusion your way
Just so he can check your faith
But one thing about it the devil can't win
If we don't involve ourselves in sin

"God don't dwell in confusion"
That's what the bible says
So when confusion starts just walk away
Because until we realize some people are just bound
Confusion will always be around

"LIFETIME PARTNERS"

A marriage is a commitment between
a woman and a man
It's a sacred event that they'll both have to plan
So before you get married and fulfill your needs
God requires you to have intimacy
Because this should be a day full of happiness and joy
So when you get married let it be for love
Both of your interest will become the same
And eventually you'll receive his last name
And since marriages are sacred and honored by God
Both you and your partner should know the man above
Because once you and your partner say "I do"
Your spirits become one even though there's two
And marriages will have their ups and downs
And problems will always come around
So when you're getting ready to plan that special date
Remember that person will be your lifetime mate

"LAST NAME"

I decided to write this poem today
To apologize for hurting you in anyway
From the first moment we touched you've always been
My lover, my confident and my best friend
You're the man I've always wanted in my life
And I knew in my heart I should've been your wife
And because I loved you and considered you my man
I took my heart and placed it in your hands
So many years has come and gone
But my feelings for you are still very strong
You're a loyal friend and that's a fact
Because there's never a time you've turned your back
And you stood by a promise that you made to me
By always being there in my time of need
At this point the only thing I can say
Is I'm sorry for hurting you and pushing you away
But now I'm ready to make a new start
That's why I'm trying to tell you what's in my heart
And I know the reason my feelings never changed
It's because I should've been carrying your last name

"CHURCH FOLK"

The bible says we'll know the last days
Because people will start behaving in strange ways
I thought Gods word suppose to make people change
But the church folk are still acting the same
If church folk would get off the seat of do nothing
They wouldn't have time to keep getting into something
Because when it comes to gossiping
church folk will talk all day
But when they're in church they won't
open their mouths and praise
And how can they claim they've been set free
When they can walk pass someone
and don't even speak?
The bible says we should love one another
So why is church folk so cruel to each other?
In Gods eyes a sin is a sin
So before judging someone else
you need to check within
Because we must realize were in the last days
And time is too short to be acting this way

"SET UP"

I let the devil set me up for the kill
By doing something that was against Gods will
I ran out of money when I came to this town
And didn't have any family or friends around
And because it was money that he knew I need
The devil sent a drug dealer to talk to me
He told me "There was only two things I could do
Either be with a man or hustle like he do"
So I chose hustling which was one of my afflictions
Never realizing it was a set up for my addiction
And one night during a party while chilling in the yard
A friend of mine asked "Did I want to play some cards"
And that was how my addiction begin
And before I knew it I was bound in sin
There was never a time that I got paid
That I didn't cash my check and gamble it away
I lost my car and got evicted from my home
And the sad thing is I didn't see nothing wrong
I had hit rock bottom and didn't know what to do
And at the same time I was hurting my children too
But there's one thing I've found to be true
If you surrender it to Jesus he'll see you through

"A CHILD'S OUTLOOK"

I remember the day my mother died
There were many reasons why I cried
When they put her in the ground I knew
I hadn't only loss a mother but a father too
My father grieved after she was gone
But that's because he had treated her wrong
But what happened in the past can't be changed
So there was no need for me to place blame
He tried to be the best father he could be
But I still felt he could've done more for me
But in order to honor my father above
I had to forgive and show my earthly father love
And I didn't worry about his health down the line
Because I keep him in prayer all the time
But now that my father is up in his years
I'm glad I was given a chance to forgive
And I pray to God every day
That the pain he's going through would go away
And even though my mother has passed and gone
I'm glad my father is still holding on
And I thank God for giving him a chance to see
The blessed outcome of his children and their seeds

"UNSELFISH"

As far as I can remember in my past
I've always put myself last
I'll always help someone if I can
But my children come before any women or man
If there was something my children wanted to do
I'd put my bills aside even though they were due
And if someone in my family ended up in jail
I would pawn something to pay their bail
And before I would see them on the street
I'd let them come and live with me
But sometimes people think I don't see
That they're using my kindness against me
But that's alright because this is who I am
And I don't expect to get my blessings from man
But don't try to use me whatever you do
Because one day you may need a blessing too

"GIFT"

There are some things you'll have to go through
Before God will birth forth a gift in you
And when things happen we don't understand
We have to look at it as part of Gods plan
Because so many things have happen to me
That people are finding hard to believe
Like how I can speak without any fear
And make it sound like I've been doing it for years
But when God places a gift in you
It'll even shock you at what you can do
Because God has appointed a time in your life
Where your gift will help someone start living right
He'll give you visions in your dreams
And only you will know what they mean
And he will already have paved the way
For what you're going to do and say
So be positioned and when the time is right
God will birth forth a gift in your life

"SOMEBODY'S CHILD"

Some people don't care about anyone else
But I don't just think about myself
We need to take the time and think for awhile
That everybody is somebody's child
Some parents teach children it's alright to fight
But they're hurting somebody's child and that's not right
And how can you go around spreading bad news
Knowing somebody's child has been hurt or confused
It's easy to go around treating people cruel
But if it was your child what would you do?
We should take the time and sympathize
And try to lift up somebody's child
God will put people in our paths everyday
To see how we treat them when they come our way
So the question I ask is "What would you do
If somebody's child was reaching out to you?

"BETRAYED"

I know that women can relate when I say
That it's a painful feeling to be betrayed
But let me clear up something that
you may have thought
Betrayal don't only happen with a boyfriend or a spouse
I started seeing signs more and more
Until they became so obvious that
they couldn't be ignored
And I tried to figure out who's the woman in his life
Because he started leaving home almost every night
But I didn't find out until the relationship ends
That I was being betrayed by one of my friends
And even though it's a man's nature
to do a woman wrong
My friend betrayed my trust because she led him on
And then they had the nerve to try to explain
But I didn't want either of them to say my name
But there's one thing that I couldn't understand
Out of all the men in the world "Why
did she pick my man?"
And now it's hard for me to ever trust again
After being betrayed by one of my friends

ABOUT THE AUTHOR

Janice Stampley Means was born in Natchez, Mississippi and currently resides in Spartanburg, S.C. She is an active member of the Bountiful Blessing Pentecostal Church under the pastorship of Thomas J. Lee.

It is an honor to present the life inspiring words of Janice S. Means. No matter what your religious beliefs, you can find shelter from confusion and sorrow from her experiences and undying faith in the healing mercy of God.

Her prose and poetry reflect the voice and tone of the Deep South as she ushers in the dynamic messages of spiritual truths. These truths of God's love and blessings are gathered from her life experiences and expressed with deep conviction. This book is a present help for all in time of spiritual need.